A Child's Book of Character Building   Book 1

God bless you as you put on Christ's Character.

Fondly,
Rebekah Coriell

A Child's Book of Character Building Book 1

Growing Up in God's World— at Home, at School, at Play

Written and Illustrated by
Ron and Rebekah Coriell

Fleming H. Revell
A Division of Baker Book House Co
Grand Rapids, Michigan 49516

© 1981 by Fleming H. Revell Company

Reprinted in paperback in 1995 by Fleming H. Revell
a division of Baker Book House Company
P.O. Box 6287, Grand Rapids, MI 49516-6287
by permission of the Association of Christian Schools International

Printed in the United States of America

ISBN 0-8007-5494-8

Scripture quotations in this volume are based on the King James Version of the Bible.

The material in this volume was excerpted from four books in the Character Builders Eyeglass Series entitled:

Listen, Look and Live
Happy Hearts
Seeing and Being Like Him
Show and Tell

Contents

FOREWORD

Introducing your children to Christ is one of the most exciting challenges facing Christian parents. Children need parental support to increasingly develop characters that reflect their faith in the living God.

A Child's Book of Character Building has been developed to help parents and children achieve this goal. These Bible stories and true-to-life situations in which children learn the meaning of godly living are designed to help boys and girls between the ages of three and seven discover how they can fulfill the plan God has for their lives.

Parents can aid their children in the use of this volume by applying it in a variety of ways. Younger children will enjoy having the book read to them, providing Mother and Father with an opportunity to explain each character trait and help the children apply it to their lives. Slightly older children may prefer to read the stories themselves and share their discoveries with the rest of the family. Or *A Child's Book of Character Building* may be a key part of family devotions as parents use the stories to spark discussions. Perhaps family members will want to tell about their opportunities to practice these traits. In family discipline parents may use previously learned character traits to guide children into behavior that pleases God. The stories they have read will help children readily grasp the twelve profound concepts covered here.

Parents across the country have found these lessons helpful in giving their children the building blocks for a happy life with Christ. We are happy to be able to provide this strong tool for building the Christian home.

THE PUBLISHERS

Attentive

Listening With the
Ears, Eyes, and Heart

My son, attend to my words;
incline thine ear unto my sayings.
Let them not depart from thine
eyes; keep them in the midst of
thine heart.

Proverbs 4:20, 21

Attentive in the Bible

"Jesus of Nazareth, thou son of David, have mercy on me," cried blind Bartimaeus. (See Mark 10:46–52.)

"Oh, be quiet, Bartimaeus. Stop calling. You're just a blind beggar," scolded people in the crowd. Bartimaeus would not be quiet.

Jesus of Nazareth was passing nearby. He had made the lame walk, healed lepers, returned the dead to life. Bartimaeus, too, wanted to be healed.

Loudly he cried out, "Thou Son of David, have mercy on me."

Through the noise of the crowd, Jesus heard and paid attention to the cries of the beggar. He stood still and commanded him to be brought to Him.

"Good news, Bartimaeus. Jesus wants to see you," said a man in the crowd.

The blind man quickly stood up and was led to Jesus.

Jesus looked at him and asked, "What do you want Me to do for you?"

"Lord, give me my sight," Bartimaeus replied.

Lovingly, Jesus answered him, "Your faith has made you well."

Immediately, he could see! Bartimaeus followed Jesus, praising God for what He had done.

Attentive at Home

"Tina, come here," called Mrs. Baker.

Oh, no! I really want to play with my doll and bottle. I'll pretend I didn't hear, thought Tina.

"Tina, come here, now!" called Mother a second time.

But Tina was not listening and continued to play. Just then, Mrs. Baker walked into the room, with a sad look on her face.

"Tina," Mother said, "Why didn't you come when I called you?"

Tina was caught. She said, "I was playing and did not want to stop. Did you want something important?"

"Tina, it is always important to come when I call," said Mother. "You must learn to listen attentively and obey."

Tina saw that her mother was sad and disappointed.

"I called you, and you chose not to obey my call," said Mother. "Jesus is very sad. He wants you to listen and obey, too."

Now Tina felt sad. "I am sorry, Mother," she said. "Will you pray with me as I ask Jesus to forgive me?"

They prayed, and then she asked her mother to forgive her, too.

Later, Mrs. Baker called Tina. This time, Tina listened and responded to her mother's call. As she ran into the kitchen to find out what Mother wanted, Mother hugged her for being prompt and attentive.

Attentive at School

Art class is Tina's favorite. The teacher, Mr. Cook, always has new and fun things to do. His students are allowed to talk quietly, while working. There is one time when Mr. Cook does not want any talking: that is when he is giving directions. He wants everyone to be attentive.

One Monday, Mr. Cook was explaining how to mix paint. Tina was trying hard to be attentive, but Alex was not. He was looking out the window. Finally, Mr. Cook finished, and the class began painting.

Tina painted a picnic scene. She mixed bright, sunny colors, just as Mr. Cook had shown her.

Alex was having trouble with his painting. He didn't know how to mix dark colors for the storm he was painting.

Tina came over to Alex's desk and asked if she could help. He said, no, it was too late. His picture was ruined.

"You could have made your stormy picture look darker by adding black to all your colors," advised Tina. "Mr. Cook showed us how. Next time, you'll have to be more attentive to the teacher."

Now Alex was sorry he had not listened or watched his teacher. He told Tina that the next time he would be attentive. And his next storm picture would be terrific.

Attentive at Play

One day, Tina's family visited a park so that they could go hiking. At the entrance, a ranger gave careful instructions. He said children should always stay with their parents. The woods were thick. It was easy to get lost or hurt. But Tina did not listen attentively as the ranger was talking.

Soon, the Baker family started on their hike through the woods. It was great fun. Tina was the last in line as they walked up and down the paths. She would stop, look, and linger. It wasn't long until her family was far ahead of her, out of sight.

She came upon a beautiful stream near the path. Tina decided to go across. She noticed some rocks in the water. They looked just big enough to step on. Slowly, she jumped from one to another. She was in the middle of the stream when she heard a noise. It was a large, strange dog. He began to bark and growl at her. Tina became so afraid that she almost slipped off the rock. Just then, a boy came running up. He chased the dog away and helped Tina get back to the bank.

Then Tina's father came running to find her. He was glad no one was hurt. He scolded Tina for not being attentive to the ranger's instructions.

Tina's family continued their hike; but, this time, Tina was the first in line.

Character Development Challenges

Attentiveness

1. Ask the child to retell a story he heard in school or church.
2. Tell how Samuel was attentive (1 Samuel 3:1–14).
3. Ask the child to list ten people to whom we should be attentive.

Faith

Believing God
Will Do What He Says

Now faith is the substance
of things hoped for, the
evidence of things not seen.

Hebrews 11:1

Faith in the Bible

The fierce wind blew against the sides of the little boat. Fighting heavy waves, the disciples rowed harder and harder. It was late at night, and they were very tired. How they wished that Jesus was with them! They remembered the time that he quieted another storm.

Knowing His disciples needed Him, Jesus went to them, walking across the water. He had faith to believe He could do this. When they saw Him, the disciples screamed with fear. Jesus told them not to be afraid.

Peter called, ". . . Lord, if it be thou, bid me come unto thee on the water" (Matthew 14:28).

Jesus told him to come. Peter climbed out of the boat and onto the angry waves. A strong wind blew against him. Frightened by the waves, Peter began to sink. He cried out, ". . . Lord, save me" (Matthew 14:30).

Jesus reached out his hand and caught Peter. "O thou of little faith," said Jesus, "why did you doubt me?" (*see* Matthew 14:31).

Peter's lack of faith prevented him from walking on the water. Jesus had the faith not only to walk on the water, but also to help Peter.

Faith at Home

One of the best times of the day, for Phil, is after supper, when the family has devotions together. They sing, memorize Bible verses, and tell how God has blessed them during the day. Father reads from the Bible, and, finally, they all pray.

One night, Phil's mother and brother visited his sick grandmother. Just Phil and his father were left to have family devotions.

First, Father sang a song to Phil about how God has promised to take care of Christians. Phil liked that song. His grandmother was a Christian. Then Father quoted from his favorite Bible verse, Romans 8:28: "All things work together for good to them that love God . . . ." Finally, Father read from the Bible, where it told about heaven.

Phil was troubled. He knew his grandmother would go to heaven if she died, but he wasn't sure he would go there. His father read, "All have sinned and come short of the glory of God. He that believeth on the Son hath everlasting life" (*see* Romans 3:23; John 6:47). That meant Phil was a sinner and needed to ask Jesus to forgive him and be his Lord and Saviour.

Phil had faith to believe Jesus would do just what He said He would. He then asked Jesus to be his Saviour. Phil was now a Christian. And if his grandmother died, he would someday see her again in heaven.

Faith at School

Phil's class was learning so much on their field trip. They learned why leaves change color in the fall. They learned why bees make honey and how clouds bring rain.

Later in the day, the wind began to blow, and the clouds grew bigger and darker. It was going to rain! Everyone raced back to the school bus.

As Phil ran, he almost stepped on something that moved in the grass. It was a baby sparrow. It had fallen out of its nest because of the wind. Phil wanted to put it back in its nest, but the tree was too high. The rain began to fall, so he left it there in the grass.

On the bus, he told Mrs. Tucker about the poor sparrow. She could tell he really cared what happened to it. Phil asked Mrs. Tucker what would happen to the baby sparrow. She said she didn't know, but she had faith to believe what God said in the Bible in Luke 12:6: ". . . not one of them is forgotten before God." God would do what He knew was best.

After the rain stopped, Phil raced back to where he had seen the sparrow. A tree limb had fallen, and its leaves covered the baby bird. There, under the protection of the leaves, the bird was dry and safe. God's eye was on that sparrow, and Phil believed God would take care of him, too!

Faith at Play

Phil's Sunday-school teacher has been telling his class how important it is to share their faith in Jesus Christ with others. Phil knew he was a Christian, but he had not thought about his friend. He wondered if José knew Jesus the way he did.

One day, after a ball game, Phil was able to ask José, "Hey, José, do you know about Jesus?" José said he did, but he didn't go to church.

As they talked, Phil explained more about Jesus. He said it is not enough to just know about Him. We must have faith in Him; that is, we must believe He will do what He says. In the Bible, He says He will forgive our sins. Jesus also says He will come into our hearts and be our Saviour if we ask Him. José had never heard that before. So Phil asked him if he would like to come to church with him the next Sunday. José said *yes*.

At Sunday school, Phil's friend listened very carefully. He began to see that Phil's words about Jesus were true.

After class, he talked to the teacher. It was then that he put his faith in what Jesus said. He asked Jesus into his heart.

Phil was so happy that he had shared his faith in Jesus. His friend had become a Christian. Now, José was looking for a friend to tell about Jesus.

Character Development Challenges

Faith

1. With the child memorize Bible verses that tell how to become a Christian (Romans 3:23; Romans 6:23; John 3:16; John 1:12).
2. Make a prayer list. Make one column for requests and another for answers.
3. List three people with whom the child could share his faith in Christ.

Creative

Doing Something in a New Way

And God saw every thing
that he had made, and,
behold, it was very good . . .

Genesis 1:31

Creative in the Bible

Many sick people were healed by Jesus. He made people who had lame legs able to walk. He made crooked hands straight. He even made dead people return to life. He was God's Son and the best doctor who ever lived.

One day, Jesus and His disciples were walking together. They saw a blind man nearby. One disciple wanted to know why this man was born blind. Jesus said His Father had planned it that way to bring glory to God. Jesus wanted to tell others about His Father in heaven. He knew people would come to be healed and would listen to His words.

Jesus could have healed this man in a very easy way, by saying, "Be healed." The man would then have been able to see. But Jesus did something in an unusual way. He spit on the ground. Then He stooped over and began to knead the wet dirt with His fingers and soon made a soft paste of mud. He put some mud on the blind man's eyes and told him to go wash his eyes in the Pool of Siloam. The blind man obeyed and came back to Jesus, able to see. He was so happy!

Why did Jesus heal the man in such a creative way? Did He want to see if the man would trust Him? The man showed that he did trust Jesus to heal him. He obeyed, and his eyes were healed.

Creative at Home

"Son, guess what?" Carl's father said. "Our friends, the Blantons, are moving. Would you like to help?"

"Sure, Father!" said Carl with excitement.

Carl likes to work, because he enjoys making work fun.

Carl was surprised when he saw all the things that had to be moved. There were chairs, books, beds, boxes, and a dog house. This was not going to be easy.

While other men were moving the furniture, he and his father moved boxes. They were very heavy, causing Carl to gasp and puff. No matter how fast he moved, it was slow work.

There must be a better way, thought Carl.

A few minutes later, he had an idea. On top of one of the heavy boxes Carl found a skateboard. He lifted the boxes onto it and pushed them to the moving van. The skateboard made moving boxes easy, fast, and fun. Before long, Carl had moved more boxes than his father.

When the job was finished, the Blantons thanked Carl and his father for their help.

Carl's father said, "You're welcome. We were happy to help."

Carl smiled inside, because of the creative idea that had made his work fun.

Creative at School

"This is going to be great! I just love to paint," said Carl.

Mrs. Dunston had announced to her class that it was art time. All the children were looking forward to painting.

"Class, today I want you to paint a picture of your choice. Do your very best and, remember, be creative!" encouraged Mrs. Dunston after passing out the art supplies.

Carl decided to paint a picture of his house. He wanted the house to be up close. The tall trees behind his house were to appear to be far away. Before he began, he just sat and thought about his painting. With his finger, he drew imaginary lines first. His teacher had told him it is very easy to erase a line you make in the air with your finger.

At last he had it planned. He was going to do it in his own special way. That's being creative.

He painted his brick house in the center of his paper and very big; that way, it looked close up. The backyard trees were painted very small, near the top of his paper. They looked far away. Then, he put in green grass, a yellow sun, and some red flowers. It was a great picture.

Mrs. Dunston thought so, too, because she said, "Carl, you are very creative."

Creative at Play

Carl loves to breathe the fresh, cold air of winter. He also likes crunching through the deep snow, in his boots.

One winter his cousin, Frank, came from Southern California to visit. Frank had never seen snow before. He and Carl had a wonderful time, running and rolling in the snow. They explored the woods in the park, and they skated on the frozen pond.

After a week of all this fun, Frank became sad. Carl asked him what was the matter. Frank said he missed the sunny beaches in California. He told Carl how he loved to build big castles in the wet sand. That gave Carl a great idea! He asked Frank if he would like to build castles in a different way.

"Sure!" said Frank.

Outside they went, with some buckets of water. Carl rolled snow into a big ball. Then, with his hands, he showed Frank how to shape a castle. They sprinkled water on the castle parts. The water froze, to make the castle solid and strong. Soon they had a castle like Frank had never seen before.

They made many creative castles that week, and Frank was as happy as he could be.

Character Development Challenges

Creativity

1. Encourage the child to draw something in a new way (a house, an animal, a car, and so forth).
2. Tell how God created the world in six days.
3. Ask the child to figure out how to help someone else in a new way.

Diligence

Working Hard
to Accomplish a Task

Seest thou a man diligent in his business? He shall stand before kings. . . .

Proverbs 22:29

Diligence in the Bible

Who could these men be, walking the streets of Jerusalem so late at night? They seemed to know each other, because they stayed together and talked quietly among themselves. One man seemed to be their leader. They made their way, past dark houses and the closed shops, toward the city gate. They walked away from Jerusalem, toward a garden called Gethsemane. As they entered the garden, Jesus asked eight men to stay behind and took three men with Him, farther in among the trees. He had often prayed in this garden, and He knew just where He wanted to speak with His heavenly Father. This night's prayer would be one of the hardest of His life.

Peter, James, and John sat down. Jesus walked farther and fell to His knees. So earnest was His prayer that blood dripped from His forehead. An hour later, He returned to His three friends, to see if they had prayed with Him. No, they had fallen asleep.

Jesus could have joined them in rest, but He had much to say to His Father. Again He prayed. He knew that soon He would be betrayed by Judas, tried, convicted, and finally crucified. Yet, Jesus worked hard to finish His second prayer. His disciples continued to sleep as Jesus diligently prayed a third time.

Our Saviour could have done many other things to prepare Himself for the dreadful events that followed; but, instead, He chose hours of diligent prayer to strengthen Himself.

41

Diligence at Home

"Can I go, too?" pleaded Danny Ellis.

His brother, Darin, responded, "No, you'd better stay home. Chopping and carrying firewood are hard work. You are too young and too little."

Danny frowned. With a hurt look in his eyes, he pulled on his father's pant leg.

"Father, I can work almost as hard as Darin. Please give me a chance," said Danny.

"All right, Son," replied Mr. Ellis. "It is hot, and the wood is heavy, so you must take it easy today."

All three climbed into the truck and drove to a farm. Mr. Ellis had been given five trees to cut down and remove. Chopping down the trees was Mr. Ellis's job. Darin cut the limbs off, and Danny was assigned to stack the wood into big piles. After two hours of work, his father and brother took a rest break, but Danny still felt strong.

"You two just take it easy. I will keep working a little longer," he insisted.

Darin and his father looked at each other in surprise. They did not think Danny would be so diligent at the hard work. The job was completed, and all the wood was stacked in the truck.

"Let's all go get a milk shake," said Mr. Ellis, winking at Darin. "I think Danny the Diligent deserves it."

Diligence at School

"I am afraid Danny is a little behind his classmates in reading," said the teacher.

"We expected this when we moved Danny to this Christian school," explained his father. "It is our hope that he will work hard to catch up to the rest of the children. Do you think you can do it, Dan?"

"I will try my best, Daddy," he replied with excitement.

Danny Ellis's new school was special. Children came from all over the city to be enrolled. Teachers and students worked together to do their best. Danny was glad to be able to attend such a school. Yet he also realized that much hard work was ahead.

Two weeks later, Danny's school had an open house. Many parents came to meet the teachers and see some of their children's work. Danny's father was especially interested in talking with Danny's teacher. "How is my son doing in his schoolwork?" Mr. Ellis asked.

With a smile of approval at Danny, the teacher replied, "Danny has had to work very hard. I am glad to report that he has become a very good reader. It is his diligence that has helped him to improve so much."

"I think Danny has become diligent since he became a Christian," responded Mr. Ellis. "Now he wants to please Jesus."

Diligence at Play

Crack! The baseball flew across the backyard. Danny's older brother, Darin, had hit another home run. With a big smile, he ran around the bases.

Now, it was Danny's turn. He gripped the bat tightly. Father pitched a ball over home plate. Danny swung with all his might, but missed the ball. Darin began to giggle.

Father cautioned, "Darin, it is not kind to giggle. You should be encouraging your younger brother. Danny, let's try it again."

With a deep sigh, Danny picked up his bat and waited for Father to pitch the ball. Tears filled his eyes.

Angrily, Danny dropped his bat and cried, "I quit!" Away he ran, to the back steps.

Father excused himself from the game and joined his son. "Son, you are not giving up, are you?" asked Father.

"I tried, but I can't hit the ball," Danny explained.

Then, Father reminded him, "Diligence means you don't give up. You must keep trying, even if you don't feel like it. The Lord is interested in your problem, Danny. Let's pray about it."

Danny asked the Lord to help him to keep trying and to have the courage he needed when it was his turn to bat.

How happy the family was to have Danny rejoin the game and diligently play baseball.

Primary Character Challenges

Diligence

1. Proverbs 6:6–8 teaches that the ant is diligent. Observe and consider an ant's life.
2. Read the story of Jacob, in Genesis 29. How did he work hard to marry his wife?
3. Romans 12:12 says, ''. . . continuing instant [diligently] in prayer.'' Find a prayer request, pray diligently, and continue until God answers your prayer.

Patience

Waiting With A Happy Spirit

Be ye also patient; stablish
your hearts. . . .

James 5:8

Patience in the Bible

Jesus' disciples were shocked at His words. They had followed the Saviour for nearly three years. They had forsaken all to serve Him. Now, He was telling them that they would soon leave Him.

Jesus said, "All ye shall be offended because of Me this night."

Peter spoke up, firmly, in protest. "Though all men shall be offended because of You, I will never be offended. Lord, I am ready to go with You, both into prison and to death."

A few hours later, Jesus was arrested, by a mob of angry men, in the Garden of Gethsemane. Just as Jesus had said, all His disciples ran away. No one stayed to help Him, not even Peter. As Jesus was taken to the high priest's house, Peter followed and joined some people warming themselves by a fire. At three different times, people told him that he looked like one of Jesus' disciples. Peter lied and denied even knowing Jesus.

As the rooster crowed a welcome to the new day, the Lord Jesus turned and looked upon Peter. Then Peter remembered the words of Jesus: "Before the cock crows you will deny Me three times."

Jesus loved Peter very much. Even though he had denied Him three times, He was willing to wait for Peter to become a faithful servant. Peter later became one of the greatest preachers of all time. The patience of Jesus was rewarded.

Patience at Home

"Mother's spaghetti!" shrieked Patty. "It's my favorite!"

Her mother smiled. "I knew you would be happy. Your father has worked very hard today, fixing the car. He is going to enjoy it, too."

Quickly, Patty ran to the backyard. She called her two younger sisters and hurriedly helped them to wash for dinner. Then they helped set the table and sat down.

"Why are we waiting?" questioned Patty.

"Well," responded Mother, "I called your father just a minute ago. He said he was coming. Let's be polite and wait patiently until everyone gets to the table."

Patty folded her hands in her lap, and so did her sisters. Mother kept working in the kitchen to prepare the last few details of the meal.

Watching the steam rise from the spaghetti, Patty thought, *I wish Father would hurry. Spaghetti is only good when it is hot.*

Moments passed that seemed like hours. Her sisters began to wiggle.

Anxiously, they asked, "May we eat now, Mother?"

"No, not until Father gets here," she said. "He will be finished soon. Please wait with happy spirits."

Just then, Father walked in with a big smile on his greasy face. "Thank you, girls," he said, "for being so patient."

Patience at School

Patty burst into the classroom. "He's bleeding, he's bleeding!" she shouted.

Startled, Mrs. Kelly jumped up from her desk and hurried into the hall. A crowd of children was standing around the drinking fountain.

"Please stand back, children. Let me have some room," she said firmly.

As the children parted, she saw Robbie, in the center, holding his mouth. Blood was trickling down between his fingers and onto the floor.

"What happened?" asked Mrs. Kelly.

"Well," said Patty, all out of breath, "We were all waiting in line for a drink. Someone at the end of the line pushed, and we all bumped into one another. Robbie was drinking and hit his tooth on the drinking fountain."

Gently wiping away the blood, Mrs. Kelly opened Robbie's mouth to see how badly his lip was cut. She carefully applied a cold towel to his lip, to prevent any swelling.

"You will be fine, Robbie," she said calmly. "There is only a small cut in your lip. Your tooth looks all right."

The children all looked at the floor when she turned to them. "We are very fortunate," she said, "that Robbie was not injured more seriously. Not being patient can cause someone to get injured. Let's remember this lesson, so that no one ever gets hurt at the drinking fountain again."

Patience at Play

I wonder if the paint is dry enough, thought Patty. *Mother said to wait until after supper.*

Circling the freshly painted swing set, she was careful not to let her dress touch the metal. How it glistened in the sun, with its shiny new coat of red paint!

Maybe, if I just touch it with one finger, she said to herself, *then I would know if it is still wet.*

Cautiously, she reached out her finger. Then, quickly, she pulled it back.

Mother said this paint only comes off with smelly paint remover. I would hate to have to wash my hands with that, thought Patty.

Again she walked around the swing, studying it closely. *I could touch it with a piece of paper,* she reasoned. *If no red paint came off, I would know that it was dry.*

Patty quickly found a stick and wrapped some old newspaper on it. Before she tried it, she changed her mind.

If the swing is still wet, the paper will stick to it and leave a mark, Patty remembered.

So, with a sigh, she decided to wait patiently until after supper. As she was helping with the dishes, her mother said, "Patty, I know it has been hard to wait with a happy spirit for the paint to dry. Because you have been so patient, you may have some ice cream when you have finished swinging."

Primary Character Challenges

Patience

1. Play a game with the child. Encourage patience as he waits for his turn.
2. Find out to whom we are to show patience. Look up Psalms 37:7 and 1 Thessalonians 5:14.
3. Help the child memorize 1 Thessalonians 5:14.

Contentment

Happy With What I Have

But godliness with contentment is great gain.

1 Timothy 6:6

Contentment in the Bible

"Master, I will follow You wherever You go." These were strange words for a scribe to say to Jesus.

A scribe was one of the few people in Bible times who knew how to read and write. He studied the Scripture and taught it to others. Some were lawyers and judges; therefore, scribes were usually wealthy, respected, and lived in nice homes.

Jesus knew that this scribe did not really mean what he said. He would not be content to live like Jesus. So the Lord replied, "The foxes have holes, and the birds have nests, but the Son of man doesn't have anywhere to lay His head."

By this, Jesus meant that even birds and animals have homes. But the Saviour didn't have a house to go home to after preaching and healing during the day. Before He came to earth, His home was in heaven. On earth, He was content to sleep outside, under the trees or in caves.

The Bible does not tell us if the scribe followed Jesus. Perhaps he was not willing to give up the nice house he lived in and sleep outside with the Master.

Jesus knew how the scribe really felt in his heart. Today, Jesus knows how happy we are with what we have. It is important that we be content, because the Bible says, "Godliness with contentment is great gain" (1 Timothy 6:6).

Contentment at Home

Connie came out of her room, with a disturbed look on her face. "Mother, I must have new shoes for school," she said.

Looking up from her dusting, Mother told Connie that her feet had not grown enough, this summer, to make new leather shoes necessary. She would have to wear last year's school shoes, because they still fit.

Connie walked back to her room, mumbling, "All the other girls will look pretty with new shoes, and I will just have these ugly old things to wear. I won't be pretty."

The night before school began, Father polished Connie's shoes. "There, they look much better," he said.

Connie still frowned. Mother reminded her that if she really wanted to look pretty for school, she would need the right spirit. "Real beauty comes from having a happy heart," she said.

The next morning, they prayed that Connie would be content with her old shoes and that she would be happy. God answered their prayer, because Connie really enjoyed her first day of school.

Mother was pleased to see her big smile as she arrived home. "I guess you were right, Mother," said Connie. "Having the right spirit makes you content. No one noticed that I didn't have new shoes."

Contentment at School

Connie frowned as she was passed a box of crayons. *These are old, broken ones,* she thought.

As she emptied the crayon box on her desk, Connie saw unbroken green and brown crayons, one-half of a blue and a yellow, and only tiny parts of red and orange crayons. None of the crayons had wrappers around them. She looked with envy at some of the other children, who had new crayons. It seemed unfair for her to get the old crayons to use. Yet she knew there were not enough new boxes of crayons to go around. This time it was her turn to use the old ones.

A Bible verse she had learned at vacation Bible school helped her to be content. She remembered that it said, "Godliness with contentment is great gain." So, without complaint, she began her drawing.

She used the green and the brown crayons to make trees and the ground. Because they did not have paper around them, she was able to use the side of the crayons to fill in the picture. The half-sized blue crayon was just large enough to color between her tree leaves, and the small yellow one was perfect for coloring small flowers. The red crayon had a jagged edge which made it easy to draw thin, red bird wings. And she used the orange to color in a bright sun.

"What a creative picture," said Miss Cooper, the teacher.

Smiling inside, Connie thought, *It really does help to be content and creative with what you have.*

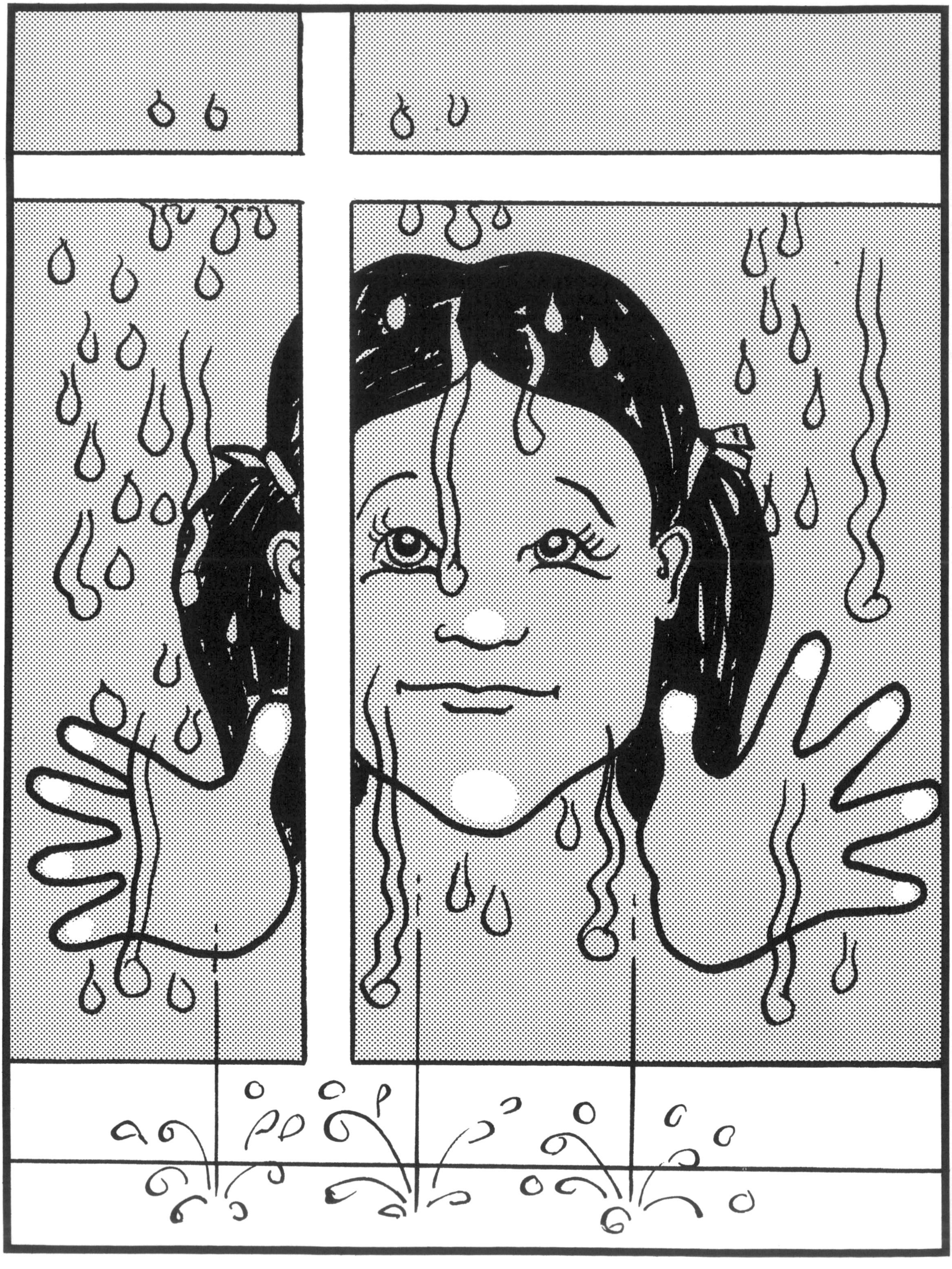

Contentment at Play

Connie jumped out of bed as the alarm clock rang. *I hope it is not raining today. Mother is taking me to the beach, to learn how to swim,* she thought.

As Connie pulled back her curtains, her joy turned to gloom. All she could see were hundreds of sparkling beads of water, running down the glass pane.

"Now, I will never be able to swim," she moaned.

Sadly, she dressed and went downstairs for breakfast. Noticing her sad spirit, her mother asked, "Why are you so gloomy today?"

"You should see the weather," Connie replied. "It is wet, dark, and cold. I just know the beach will be closed."

"I know you are unhappy," said Mother, "but you can't let this make you sad all day. You must be content to not swim today. Maybe tomorrow will be sunny."

As the family ate breakfast, Connie's father talked about how Jesus was happy with what He had. He left the beauty of heaven and was content to be born in a stable. He could have been a king, but He was happy as a servant to others. He could have lived in a mansion; however, He was content to never own a house.

Connie wanted to be like Jesus. With a smile, she said, "I will be content and happy, even if I can't learn to swim today."

Primary Character Challenges

Contentment

1. Teach the child to find blessings in an area in which he is not content.
2. Help the child memorize 1 Timothy 6:6.
3. List the things that God promises will last for eternity, in the following verses: Isaiah 40:8, Matthew 6:19-21, Psalms 90:2, and Hebrews 13:8.

Obedience

Doing What You Are Told
With a Happy, Submissive Spirit

Obey them that have the
rule over you . . . .
Hebrews 13:17

.

Obedience in the Bible

Once a year, the family of Jesus traveled to the city of Jerusalem to celebrate a special Jewish holiday called Passover. Jesus, a boy of twelve, went with them. When the feast ended seven days later, Mary and Joseph prepared to return home. They were traveling with many others, in a caravan, to be protected from robbers. His parents thought that Jesus was with them, but He was still in Jerusalem. It was a whole day before they discovered that He was gone.

Quickly they returned to Jerusalem. His parents began to look everywhere. At last someone directed them to the Jewish temple. There they found Jesus, sitting and talking to the teachers, who were amazed at His wisdom and knowledge of the Old Testament. His parents asked Him why He had not come with them. He answered that He must be about His heavenly Father's business. They did not understand this, but Jesus happily obeyed His earthly parents and returned with them to His home in Nazareth.

The Bible says Jesus was subject unto them. That means He did what He was told with a happy and obedient spirit. The Bible also says, "Jesus increased in wisdom . . ." (Luke 2:52). It is wise to obey.

Obedience at Home

"Hey, Mike," shouted Billy. "Look what I found!"

Mike glanced up from playing in his yard, to see his friend Billy climbing out on a limb of the old maple tree.

"It looks like a robin's nest. Do you want me to show you the eggs?" said Billy.

"Didn't your father tell you not to climb that tree?" Mike responded.

"Well, yes," answered Billy. "I'll be careful. I'll put the eggs back before he gets home. Besides, you took four robin's eggs to school last week."

"I know I did, but didn't you hear what happened?" Mike replied.

"No, what happened?" asked Billy, as he stopped climbing just before reaching the nest.

"I was so proud of my robin's eggs that I showed them to everyone," explained Mike. "One of the eggs dropped when I was showing them to my friends. Two more were broken when I fell while riding my bike."

Mike continued, "Later, when my father found out, he had me place the remaining egg back in the nest and watch it. The mother robin wouldn't go near it. Father told me that birds will never return to their eggs when they have been touched by people."

"So that's why my father told me to stay away from our robin's nest!" Billy thought aloud.

"I had better climb down," Billy concluded. "There are many reasons why it is wise to obey Father's rules."

Obedience at School

A voice over the intercom asked Mrs. Harper, Billy's teacher, to go to the office. She told the class to remain quiet and finish their work.

Now is my chance to make the paper airplane that Billy showed me, thought Jeff. As Mrs. Harper left the room, Jeff started to fold a piece of paper into a plane.

Billy looked at his friend Jeff and was surprised. He thought, *Jeff just accepted Christ as his Saviour, at church Sunday. He should not be disobeying the teacher.*

Jeff had finished folding his paper airplane and was ready to fly it.

"Hey, Jeff," whispered Billy.

"What?" answered Jeff.

"Now that you are a Christian, you ought to know a special Bible verse. It has helped me to do right," explained Billy.

"All right, what is it?" asked Jeff.

Billy recited Proverbs 15:3: " 'The eyes of the Lord are in every place, beholding the evil and the good.' That means God is watching everything we do, wherever we are."

Jeff thought for a moment. Then he put the airplane in his desk and smiled at Billy.

"Thanks for helping me to do what we were told," said Jeff. "You are a real Christian friend."

Obedience at Play

"Oh, no! It's stuck!" exclaimed Billy.

Billy had just hit a softball so high that it almost went over the roof of the shed. It hit the peak of the roof and rolled down into the gutter.

Billy loves to play softball. He can play it any time of the day and all day, if his mother lets him. One thing she will not let him do is climb up the shed roof. It is dangerous, she says, and his father has told him that he must call for help if a ball ever gets caught up there.

"Now, what are we going to do?" a friend complained.

"Well, we will have to do what my father told me to do," answered Billy. "Go for help."

Off he ran to find his father. The other boys shook their heads. They didn't understand why he couldn't just sneak up on the roof. Who would find out?

Billy came back with his father and a ladder. In a jiffy, the ball was retrieved.

Billy's father was so glad that his son had obeyed his wise words. As a reward, he decided to join the boys in their game of softball. Now, even Billy's friends are glad he obeyed.

Character Development Challenges

Obedience

1. The parent or teacher should make a chart which children can mark using stars or stickers to show when they have obeyed.
2. With the child, discover a Bible character who disobeyed and tell what happened to him.
3. Teach the child to sing the hymn "'Trust and Obey."

Wisdom

Thinking God's Way

Wisdom is the principal thing;
therefore get wisdom. . . .

Proverbs 4:7

Wisdom in the Bible

The Jews lived in a land ruled by the Romans, who did not believe in God. The Jews hated their Roman rulers; some Jews also hated Jesus. The religious leaders did not believe Jesus was God's Son. They sent spies to try to trick Him.

These men came to Jesus with a special question. They asked Him if it were right for the Jews to pay taxes to the Romans. They hoped that He would answer *yes* or *no*. If He said *yes*, the Jews would be angry with Jesus. If He said *no*, the Romans would be angry with Him.

Jesus was a wise man. He always thought the thoughts of God, His Father. His answer was not *yes* or *no*.

Jesus said, "Show Me the tribute money."

So they brought Him a penny.

"Whose image is this?" asked Jesus.

They answered, "Caesar's, the Roman ruler."

Then Jesus said that they should give Caesar the things that belong to Caesar and give to God the things that belong to God.

Jesus had answered very wisely; no one could be angry with Him. When the spies returned to the Jewish religious leaders, they had nothing evil to report.

Wisdom at Home

Everyone in Wendy's family was sad. Father was going on a business trip. He would be gone a whole week.

Father reminded Wendy that she must be her mother's helper. Kissing everyone good-bye, he promised to telephone the following night. Everyone was sad to see him go, but it made them happy to know that he would call them soon.

The next day, everyone waited for the phone to ring. At last, it did. Mother answered. It was Father! Wendy's younger brother, Peter, became so excited that he started to cry. Wendy knew Mother could not hear Father's words, with all of Peter's crying. She knew that God's Word says, "Be ye kind one to another . . ." (Ephesians 4:32). She was sure it would please God if she played with Peter and helped keep him quiet, so she did. Mother and Father talked a long time, and Wendy had to give up her turn to talk.

When the call was over, Mother called Wendy. She said, "Wendy, you are such a wise girl. You helped me to hear Father's voice."

Wendy said she knew what God had wanted her to do. And it made her so happy to know her mother was pleased.

After Peter was tucked into bed, Wendy and Mother shared a plate of cookies and some milk, and Mother told her what Father had said.

Wisdom at School

One Tuesday the weather was very hot. The principal decided it would be a special treat to have a school picnic. At lunchtime, all the children went outside to eat. It was such fun. Wendy and Samantha found a nice tree to sit under. The shade made it cool. When they finished, they decided to take a short walk in the school yard.

Just then, a strange man called to them. "Hey, girls, come here. I have something to give you."

Wendy had never seen him before. Samantha wondered if he might have candy in the bag.

"Let's go and see what he has," said Samantha.

She started to go toward him, but Wendy grabbed her arm.

"Mother told me never to talk to strangers," Wendy said. "We had better tell our teacher about him."

Mrs. Weber was so glad to hear how wisely the girls had acted.

"I know that God was very pleased that you obeyed the advice of Wendy's mother. Some strangers are not kind and might hurt you," said Mrs. Weber.

After hearing her words, Wendy and Samantha were very glad that they had been wise.

Wisdom at Play

Wendy's face was so sad. She looked out the window. All she could see was rain. It had rained all week. She wanted to play outside. She was tired of playing in her room. There were no more books to read, and all the table games had been played. She was even tired of listening to records.

Wendy went to her mother and sadly asked, "What can we do different today?"

Mother had a great idea. Father had just cleaned out the garage. She said they could play in there. Wendy shouted with glee! She and her brother, David, could even ride their bikes. Mother moved the car and told Wendy to watch David. Wendy said she would. Around and around they went on their bikes. They were having so much fun!

While they were playing, David picked up a bright-red can. Wendy knew this was Father's gas can, and it was very dangerous. Wendy knew God was watching her, to see what she would do. She also knew He wanted her to act wisely. So she decided to take the gas can away from her brother. She put it on a high shelf. Of course David cried, but she was happy she had done the right thing.

Father came home later that evening. He asked Wendy where his gas can was. She then told him what had happened. Her father smiled and gave both Wendy and David a big hug. In his heart, he thanked God for a wise daughter like Wendy.

Character Development Challenges

Wisdom

1. Help the child memorize some Bible verses about wisdom (Psalms 111:10; Proverbs 4:7; James 1:5; Proverbs 24:3, 4; Proverbs 3:13).
2. The child should draw a picture of someone demonstrating wisdom.
3. The child should find out and tell how Solomon received his wisdom (1 Kings 3:3–14; 2 Chronicles 1:7–12).

Tenderhearted

Strong Enough to Feel
the Joys and Hurts of Others

Be ye kind one to another,
tenderhearted . . . .
Ephesians 4:32

Tenderhearted in the Bible

As Jesus and His disciples were approaching the small village of Nain, they were halted by a funeral procession coming through the city gate.

"My son, my only son," mourned a widow as the body passed Jesus and His followers. Many mourners were following from the city.

When Jesus saw the mother, His heart overflowed with sympathy for her.

"Weep not," He said to her.

Then Jesus walked over and touched the casket. Looking in at the young man, He said, "Arise."

There was a great stir among the crowd when the young man sat up and began to talk! Jesus took him to his mother and reunited him with the rejoicing woman.

Jesus, tenderly, felt sorry for this widow. He was so moved by her great sorrow that He brought her only son back to life again.

Tenderhearted at Home

Tommy's grandpa lived next door. Tommy loved to help Grandpa do all sorts of jobs. They raked leaves, washed the car, and even fished together.

One hot July day, Grandpa was mowing the lawn. The family reunion was to be at Grandpa's house. All the nieces, nephews, cousins, aunts, and uncles were coming. Grandpa wanted the yard to look neat.

As Tommy watched Grandpa mow the lawn, he noticed how hot and tired Grandpa was getting.

I wish there were something special that I could do to help Grandpa. There is only one lawn mower. And he is using it, thought Tommy. *I've got an idea!*

He ran into the house. A few minutes later, he came out with an ice-cold glass of lemonade. Grandpa was so tired that he had sat down on a rock and was wiping his brow with a handkerchief. Tommy offered him the lemonade.

Grandpa was very pleased that Tommy had been so tender. He was able to finish mowing the lawn because tenderhearted Tommy had cared.

Tenderhearted at School

"Ouch, ouch, ouch!" cried Victor.

"Are you all right?" asked Tommy. "That must have really hurt."

Tommy's friend Victor had stumbled and fallen while playing tag on the school playground. His hand was scraped and dirty. Tommy saw how skinned Victor's hand looked, and he knew it needed quick attention. So he told Victor to go see Miss MaryAnn.

Everyone likes Miss MaryAnn, the school nurse. She is so kind and gentle. But no one likes to get a hurt hand.

"Oh, no! Not me!" Victor protested.

He was afraid that what the nurse might put on his hand would hurt worse than the scrape.

Tommy begged him to be brave and go anyway. It was best to get his hand taken care of properly, or later it would hurt even more. Tommy sensed that Victor needed to be encouraged.

"Look, I'll go with you. Maybe it won't seem so bad if we go together," said Tommy.

Victor agreed, and both went to the school clinic.

It took Miss MaryAnn only five minutes to clean Victor's hand and put a bandage on. And it didn't even hurt.

Victor was glad he had a friend like Tommy, who was tenderhearted and knew how he felt.

Tenderhearted at Play

"It sure must be tough for Ike to sit all day in that wheelchair," said Tommy as his neighborhood soccer team passed Ike's house.

"Why can't he walk?" asked Joey.

"Before you moved here, Ike hurt himself while diving into a swimming pool," Tommy said.

The boys walked on toward the soccer field. Tommy looked back at Ike. He could see a frown on his face. Ike was sad that he had no one to play with.

Tommy remembered last summer, when his leg was in a cast. He could not run or play, so he had to learn to play quiet games, such as checkers.

Maybe Ike would like to play checkers, thought Tommy. *But what will my friends say? Will they call me a sissy? Will they laugh at me?*

Tommy looked at his friends. He looked at Ike. Then Tommy said, "Joey, you and the boys go play soccer. I am going to visit Ike."

Tommy went back to Ike's house. "Hi, Ike," said Tommy. "How would you like to play checkers?"

"Boy, would I!" said Ike, as Tommy came up the porch steps. "I was hoping that someone would play with me."

Tommy felt good inside, because he understood Ike's loneliness. Being tenderhearted, he was strong enough to make the right choice.

Character Development Challenges

Tenderheartedness

1. Ask the child to cut out magazine pictures of people who need tenderheartedness.
2. Help the child act out the Bible story of the widow of Nain, found in Luke 7:11–17.
3. With the child, list five people to be tenderhearted toward and tell how to demonstrate this quality to them.

Thankfulness

Being Grateful
and Saying So

In every thing give thanks: for this is the will of God in Christ Jesus concerning you.

1 Thessalonians 5:18

Thankfulness in the Bible

Mary of Bethany had entered the room in which Jesus and His disciples sat at dinner in Simon the leper's house. She opened an alabaster box and slowly poured its costly contents upon Jesus' head. As the smell of this perfume filled the room, Mary poured some on Jesus' feet and began to wipe them with her long hair.

The disciples of Jesus were very angry. "Why are you wasting this ointment?" Judas shouted. "Why wasn't it sold for fifty dollars and the money given to the poor?"

Jesus realized that there was deep meaning behind what Mary was doing. He said, "Let her alone. For she has done a good work for Me. For ye have the poor always with you, but you will not always have Me. She has poured this ointment on My body for My burial."

Jesus had often told His followers that He would soon die. They could not understand this, but Mary understood. The ointment she had poured on Jesus was one that people used when they buried the dead.

Gratefully, Jesus smiled as Mary finished drying His feet. He was thankful for her kindness and for her understanding. He said, "Verily I say unto you, wheresoever the gospel shall be preached, in the whole world, what this woman has done will be told as a memorial to her."

Thankfulness at Home

"Oh, no, not again," moaned Mr. Williams. "All the water in the radiator is boiling out. We can't go any farther unless we get some water."

The family sat in sadness, watching steam pour out from under the hood.

"It's getting dark, and I don't see any houses on this road. What shall we do?" asked Hank.

Reassuringly, Mother replied, "We will just have to sit and wait for help."

As the family waited, the wind began to blow, and dark clouds swirled overhead. Suddenly, Father jumped out of the car and ran back to the trunk. He lifted out an ice chest and some pots and pans. He placed them on the shoulder of the road. Heavy rain came down, just as he got back in the car. Everyone was thankful to be inside.

The storm lasted for thirty minutes. When it was over, everyone got out to inspect how well Father's idea had worked. Just as he had hoped, enough water had been collected in all the containers.

"After I fill the radiator, we'll be able to travel," Mr. Williams announced. "But, first, let's all thank God for sending us a big rainstorm. What a special way He chose to help meet our need tonight."

Thankfulness at School

"I am so tired today," sighed Hank, after school.

"Me, too," agreed Larry.

"Mrs. Clark is a good substitute teacher, but I really miss our teacher, Mrs. Mart," said Hank.

"You can say that again, Hank," responded Larry. "Remember how kind she is? She always has such a cheerful hello for everyone. She makes us feel so important. Will Mrs. Mart be back tomorrow?"

"I don't know. I learned a good lesson, while she was away, today," replied Hank.

"What lesson is that?" asked Larry.

"Well," said Hank, "we have enjoyed Mrs. Mart as a teacher. I have always been thankful for her, but I've never told her so."

With a sad look, Larry replied, "Neither have I. It is important to be grateful. And it is just as important to say you appreciate someone."

"How can we do that?" asked Hank.

"Maybe we could tell her as soon as she gets back to school," suggested Larry.

Hank thought a moment and then said, "Let's send her a get-well card. We'll tell her how thankful we are that she is our teacher. And let's say we are praying that she will get well very soon."

Thankfulness at Play

"Mother, I am so bored with these toys. I wish I had new ones," complained Hank.

"Your birthday was last month," replied Mother. "Aren't you content with the new ones that you received?"

"I like all my toys," sighed Hank, "but I am tired of them."

Mother put down her dustcloth and sat on the ottoman, in front of Hank. "Do you remember the slides we saw Sunday, at church?" she asked. "Our missionaries told us about some poor children. Do you remember that he said most of the children had to make their own toys? Do you think those children would be grateful if they had just a few of your toys?"

Hank thought a moment and answered, "I know they would be happy with even *one* of my toys. I have not been as thankful as I should be. Would Jesus understand if I asked Him to forgive me for being so ungrateful?"

"Yes, He would," assured his mother.

"And I think," said Hank, "that I had better tell Jesus, right now, how thankful I am for all the toys He has given to me."

Primary Character Challenges

Thankfulness

1. Encourage a child to exhibit a spirit of thankfulness by having him create an appreciation card and mail it to someone who has been kind to him.
2. Teach the child the principle of "In every thing give thanks . . ." (1 Thessalonians 5:18), by having him relate some recent, unpleasant experiences in which he had to be thankful.
3. Guide the child into developing a spirit of thankfulness by having him memorize Psalms 100:4: "Enter into his gates with thanksgiving. . . ."

Honesty

Truthful Words and Ways

Wherefore putting away ly-
ing, speak every man truth
with his neighbor. . . .

Ephesians 4:25

Honesty in the Bible

"Peter, James, John, rise up. Let us go," said Jesus.

Everything had been very quiet that Passover evening in the Garden of Gethsemane. Now the gentle hush of the trees was broken by the sounds of footsteps and rustling leaves. Lighted torches, carried by soldiers and angry men, could be seen around Jesus and His disciples. Some of the soldiers were carrying swords.

Jesus knew the mob was coming to arrest Him. It would mean suffering and death for Him. He could see Judas coming. How deeply it hurt to know that His friend was going to betray Him with a kiss. Aware of these dangers, yet unafraid, Jesus resisted any temptation to run or hide.

He faced the angry crowd. He asked, "Whom are you seeking?"

"Jesus of Nazareth," the crowd replied.

Jesus' character could only give an honest answer: "I am He." His truthful words shocked the mob so that they fell to the ground.

Again, He questioned them, "Whom are you seeking?"

"Jesus of Nazareth," the mob answered again.

"I am He. Let My disciples go," Jesus replied.

With great strength and courage, Jesus honestly faced the mob.

Honesty at Home

"Juan, now you are in big trouble," said his friend Harold. "The airplane is broken."

The boys had been playing in the den. Juan had climbed on a chair to reach a large model airplane he wanted to show Harold. It slipped out of his fingers and plunged to the floor, breaking the right wing.

Harold was afraid and asked, "Aren't you going to run?"

"Let's go," replied Juan. "Maybe Father will think the cat knocked it off."

The rest of the day, Juan's conscience bothered him. God was telling him to tell the truth about the plane. Verses of Scripture ran through his mind: ". . . be sure your sin will find you out. The eyes of the Lord are in every place beholding the evil. . . . Speak ye every man the truth. . . ."

Time passed slowly as Juan waited for his father to come home. Hearing the car in the driveway, he greeted his father at the front door. "Dad, can I talk to you alone?" asked Juan.

He led his father to the den. When Mr. Cortez saw the wrecked plane, he was surprised and disappointed.

"I dropped it, Father," said Juan. "It slipped from my fingers as I was showing it to Harold."

"I would have had a broken heart if you had not told me," said Father. "Thank you, Son, for being honest with me."

Honesty at School

"I am happy to announce that the winner of the art contest is Juan Cortez!" reported Mr. Higdon, the principal.

It can't be true, Juan thought. *I rushed to complete my picture. It can't be good enough to win.*

As Mr. Higdon shook Juan's hand, he proudly pointed to Juan's prize-winning painting. Juan's eyes grew as big as golf balls. The picture to which Mr. Higdon pointed was not his. It really belonged to Bentley Brown.

Many questions ran through Juan's mind: *What shall I do? Why was my name on the picture? How did it happen? Everyone knows Bentley is the best artist in the class. There are students in the class who do not like Bentley. I wonder if they switched my name with his, so that he wouldn't win.*

Juan had always been truthful in his words and ways. That was being like Jesus. Now he had the opportunity to show others that being honest was more important to him than winning the contest. Motioning to Mr. Higdon, he whispered the truth in the principal's ear.

"Thank you, Juan, for being so honest," said Mr. Higdon. "I will correct the mistake right now."

Juan felt a little disappointment as he handed the winner's ribbon to Bentley Brown. But he was sure that he had made the right decision. He knew he had pleased Jesus, too.

115

Honesty at Play

"Father, could you give me some advice?" asked Juan.

"Sure, Son," replied Mr. Cortez.

"My friend Francis is not liked by any of the neighborhood boys. It is so hard to be his friend," Juan said.

"Why don't they like Francis?" asked Father.

"The truth is," answered Juan, "that he looks and smells dirty. My friends just don't want to play with him."

"Are you being friendly to him?" his father asked.

"Sometimes, Father," said Juan. "But he must think that I would rather play with the other boys, instead of him."

"Is that true?" asked Mr. Cortez.

Embarrassed, Juan admitted, "I guess so."

Then Father tenderly lifted Juan onto his lap. He reminded him that Jesus tried to help people who were despised. He encouraged Juan to try to help Francis.

"But how?" pleaded Juan.

"By being honest and telling him the truth. In a kind way, you must tell him that being dirty makes other people unfriendly. Then pray that God will help him to change," replied Father.

The next morning, Juan was honest with Francis about his problem. Francis went home, bathed, and changed his clothes. Juan's honesty helped him make a good friend.

Primary Character Challenges

Honesty

1. Being true to one's word is a valuable character trait to develop in a child. Whenever your child makes a promise, be sure to explain the importance of honesty and following through on his word.
2. Have the child memorize Ephesians 4:25 and explain its meaning.
3. Remind the child to avoid exaggeration, which is a form of dishonesty. Have him memorize Romans 12:17: ". . . Provide things honest in the sight of all men."

Joyfulness

Being Happy
Inside and Out

And my soul shall be joyful in
the Lord: it shall rejoice in his
salvation.

Psalms 35:9

Joyfulness in the Bible

"Go away! The Master doesn't have time for children," snapped the disciples.

Disappointedly, the mothers and fathers reached out to claim the little children they had brought to have Jesus bless. They had hoped He would place His hands on them. Instead, the disciples pushed them away.

Jesus' tender eyes saw the disappointed faces of the children and their parents. Compassionately He called, "Let the little children come to Me. Forbid them not, for of such is the kingdom of heaven."

Then, Jesus lifted up the little children in His arms and held them. It gave Him joy to know that someday He would have children of all ages with Him in heaven.

It was this joy that made Him willing to endure the cross and its shame. He could rejoice with confidence, because He was going to be obedient to death on the cross; therefore, God's children would live with Him forever.

Jesus promised the disciples that His joy would remain in them, if they obeyed God's commandments. If we obey, His joy will be in us, too.

Joyfulness at Home

Saturday was one of those days when everything seemed to go wrong. It was a test of Jenny Henson's ability to stay joyful.

Jenny got up late. She took a quick bath and dressed. Because she had trouble finding her shoes, her breakfast was cold. She gulped down her eggs and ran out the door, to catch her ride to day camp.

Although she ran all the way to the church, she was still late. When she arrived at the parking lot, she discovered that the bus had just left. Jenny wanted to cry. Her day was such a disappointment. Then her thoughts turned to Jesus and His disappointments on earth.

He was the Creator; the people He made hated Him. Lowly shepherds worshiped Him at His birth; and He was spit upon by soldiers, at His death. For three long years, He trained His disciples, only to have them run away when He was arrested.

"Jesus must surely know how I feel right now," she said aloud. "I'm not going to let my disappointing morning take away my joy."

Jenny took a deep breath and started walking home. She rejoiced as she thought that ". . . all things work together for good to them that love God, to them who are the called according to His purpose" (Romans 8:28).

Joyfulness at School

Have you ever had your heart set on something you really wanted to do? That was the way Jenny felt, in gym class. She wanted to play on the trampoline. She loved to flip in the air. Last week, she had learned to touch her toes while being in the air.

Excitedly, Jenny dressed in her gym clothes, hoping to be the first in line for the trampoline. The girls lined up as Mrs. Best, the gym teacher, blew the whistle. Then, to Jenny's surprise, Mrs. Best asked the girls to choose the game that they wanted to play. Kickball was their favorite game.

Oh, but that is not as much fun, Jenny almost shouted. *It is going to be hard to be happy playing kickball, but I will try,* she thought.

Smiling, she entered into the kickball game. Soon, her smile on the outside helped her to be happy inside, too.

When the game was over, Mrs. Best announced that Jenny's classroom teacher had to leave school early. The class would be staying in gym until school was dismissed. They could have a free period to use any of the gym equipment. As Jenny raced to the trampoline, she thought, *God sometimes has surprises for us, when we are joyful in all things.*

Joyfulness at Play

"Jenny," said her mother, "your cousin, Sally, is coming to stay with us for a month."

"Oh, that is wonderful. Now, I will have someone my age to play with," responded Jenny.

Jenny's excitement grew as the day came nearer. She had all kinds of activities planned. They would hike, swim, and catch butterflies. And they could play badminton with her new set. However, these dreams faded when her cousin was brought home from the bus station. Sally recently had been crippled in a car accident and had to walk with special braces on her legs.

Jenny smiled on the outside as she greeted Sally. On the inside, she was sad. She felt sorry for Sally and for herself. Her cousin did not let her problem make her sad. She was cheerful and ready to try anything.

As the weeks went by, with a little help, Sally joyfully swam in the pool. She hiked with Jenny, as long as they walked slowly. Sally became fairly good at catching butterflies with a net. And she could even play badminton.

Sally's cheerfulness made Jenny feel joyful, too. She never would forget her joyful cousin. And God helped Jenny to remember that it is best to have a happy spirit.

Primary Character Challenges

Joyfulness

1. John 15:10, 11 says that obedience is a key to joyfulness. Discuss with the child five ways in which he can become joyful by obeying.
2. Psalms 63:5, 6 instructs us to praise the Lord with joyful words, by meditating with Him each evening before going to sleep. Review Bible verses which speak about joy and use them at bedtime.
3. Assist the child in memorizing Philippians 2:14. Explain how the child can be joyful in what he does.